# DRAMATIC CRITICISM

# DRAMATIC CRITICISM

THREE LECTURES DELIVERED
AT THE ROYAL INSTITUTION
FEBRUARY 1903

BY

## A. B. WALKLEY

LONDON
JOHN MURRAY, ALBEMARLE STREET
1903

# CONTENTS

## PART I

## PART II

## PART III

# I

## THE IDEAL SPECTATOR

# DRAMATIC CRITICISM

## I

IT is not to be gainsaid that the word
" criticism " has gradually acquired a certain
connotation of contempt. Indeed, one is
sometimes tempted to wish that " criticism " and " critic " could be expunged from
the dictionary, so lamentably misused as
they are. Every one who expresses opinions,
however imbecile, in print calls himself a
" critic." The greater the ignoramus, the
greater the likelihood of his posing as a
" critic." The title has become as vulgar as
" Professor," which Matthew Arnold mod-
estly declined to share with Professor
Pepper. But vulgarity, as we know, is
sometimes a very different thing from
popularity. It is significant that the voca-
bulary of daily life has never adopted the
word " critic " as a term of endearment.

From the people whom the critic criticises it would be unreasonable to expect sympathy. When the rowdy baronet in Mr. Pinero's play felt particularly lively he always broke a valuable piece of porcelain, and it is an infallible sign of exuberant health in a popular actor when he says something sarcastic about the dramatic critics. There is a story in Bret Harte—or in Mark Twain—of a youthful convalescent in San Francisco about whom anxious inquirers were reassured by the information that " he was quite peart-like, heavin' rocks at the Chinamen." What the Chinamen were to this interesting invalid, the dramatic critics are to the popular actor — *hostes humani generis* — the mark for rocks, or any more handy missile. The dramatic critic's fellow-playgoers regard him as a wet blanket, a spoil-sport. They " know what they like," as the phrase goes, and therefore they look askance at the man one of whose functions it is to persuade them that they do not know what they ought to like. This attitude has been illustrated in a question seriously debated by a club of

playgoers—"Are Dramatic Critics of any
use?" But critics have been most sorely
stricken in the house of their friends, that
is to say, by authors and other critics.
You have Dryden in the dedication of his
"Examen Poeticum" declaring that "the
corruption of a poet is the generation of a
critic"—though here the whirligig of time
has brought in his revenges, for Dryden
himself is less rarely read to-day for his
criticism than for his poetry. You have
another critic, Addison, filling a whole
*Spectator* paper with sarcasms against the
dramatic critics. You have a third critic,
Dr. Johnson, devoting two papers in
the *Idler* to the satirical picture of the
dramatic critic Dick Minim, and remarking
that "Criticism is a study by which we
grow important and formidable at a very
small expense." The favourite, the classical, theory, however, of literary persons
is that the critic is an author *manqué*.
Coleridge said reviewers were "Usually
people who would have been poets, his-
torians, biographers, if they could; they
have tried their talents at one or the other

and have failed ; therefore they turn critics."
Shelley said : "As a bankrupt thief turns
thief-taker in despair, so an unsuccessful
author turns critic." Landor, in an Imaginary Conversation, made Porson tell
Southey : "Those who have failed as
writers turn reviewers." Balzac greatly
vexed Saint-Beuve by saying of an unsuccessful sculptor that "il passa critique
comme tous les impuissants qui mentent à
leurs débuts." In the same strain you have
Lord Beaconsfield's epigram in "Lothair,"
"Who are the critics? Those who have
failed in literature and art."

Well, all this is very depressing, and, to
recover a little tone, the critic naturally
adopts the attitude of Shylock in the speech
wherein he demonstrated to the Christians
that he was a man and a brother. What
people forget is that in this matter of criticism we are all tarred with the same brush.
Just as one solid body cannot collide with
another without the manifestation of a form
of energy which we call heat, so one mind
cannot impinge upon another without the
manifestation of that form of energy which

we call criticism.  Criticism is the means
whereby art becomes conscious of its existence.  Survey the playhouse and take a
rapid poll of the audience.  The million-
aire in the stage box is politely stifling a
yawn behind his kid-glove; Miss in the
stalls is whispering to her Mamma that
Sir Toby Belch seems very tipsy, and that
anyhow it isn't half so funny as *Charley's
Aunt*.  The pit are shuffling their feet,
and the gallery-boy is shouting "boo!"
They are all "undulant and diverse," as
Montaigne would say, and yet the whole
audience have one thing in common; they
are all dramatic critics — of the species
known as "impressionist."  As M. Jour-
dain spoke prose, so they are all producing
criticism, without knowing it.

Still there is, of course, criticism and
criticism, a right criticism and a wrong;
criticism according to knowledge and good
taste and criticism according to neither;
the criticism of the *habiles* and the criticism of the *simples*, to use La Bruyère's
classification.  It must be our task to reduce, if we can, this chaos of opinion to

something like order, and to put our finger on the best opinion, the opinion of what we may call the ideal spectator. It is to this ideal spectator that the drama, as an art—we are not concerned here with the drama as merchandise, for that, no doubt, often finds itself addressed to a very different destination—it is to this ideal spectator that the drama as an art is addressed. Aristotle, the earliest and still the greatest of dramatic critics, made a great point of this ideal spectator. You will remember that it was Mr. Borthrop Trumbull, the auctioneer in "Middlemarch," who conjectured that "the old masters were probably so called because they knew a thing or two more than the young 'uns." This remark is certainly true about Aristotle, the oldest master, *il maestro di color che sanno*, the master of those who know. "As in ethics," says Professor Butcher,[1] "Aristotle assumes a man of moral insight (ὁ φρόνιμος) to whose trained judgment the appreciation of ethical questions is

[1] "Aristotle's Theory of Poetry and Fine Art," 2nd ed., p. 209.

submitted, and who, in the last resort, becomes the 'standard and the law' of right, so too in fine art a man of sound æsthetic interests (ὁ χαρίεις) is assumed, who is the standard of taste, and to him the final appeal is made." Now there is no need for playgoers to rise up and "conspuer" this ideal spectator—ὁ χαρίεις. We need none of us be in any hurry to hate him and abuse him as though he had robbed a church. For the fact is, he does not exist. He is like a point in pure geometry, an abstract conception. We call him the ideal spectator, or reader, or listener, just because he is not real. But he furnishes a convenient standard by which we can classify the tastes of real spectators, or readers, or listeners, and the nearest approximation to him will furnish us with our best opinion. To fix your ideas, to give yourselves an instance of an actual approximation to the character of Aristotle's χαρίεις, I think you cannot choose anything much better than Hazlitt's description of his friend Joseph Fawcett:—

"We find people of a decided and origi-

nal, and others of a more general and
versatile, taste.  I have sometimes thought
that the most acute and original-minded
men made bad critics.  They see everything
too much through a particular medium.
What does not fall in with their own bias
and mode of composition strikes them as
commonplace and factitious. . . . The
extreme force of their original impressions
compared with the feebleness of those they
receive at second-hand from others, over-
sets the balance and just proportion of
their minds.  Men who have fewer native
resources, and are obliged to apply oftener
to the general stock, acquire by habit a
greater aptitude in appreciating what they
owe to others.  Their taste is not made a
sacrifice to their egotism and vanity, and
they enrich the soil of their minds with
continual accessions of borrowed strength
and beauty.  I might take this opportunity
of observing, that the person of the most
refined and least contracted taste I ever
knew was the late Joseph Fawcett, the
friend of my youth.  He was almost the
first literary acquaintance I ever made, and

I think the most candid and unsophisticated.
He had a masterly perception of all styles
and of every kind and degree of excellence,
sublime or beautiful, from Milton's 'Paradise Lost' to Shenstone's 'Pastoral Ballad,'
from Butler's 'Analogy' down to 'Hum-
phrey Clinker.' If you had a favourite
author, he had read him too, and knew all
the best morsels, the subtle *traits*, the capital
touches. 'Do you like Sterne?'—'Yes, to
be sure,' he would say. 'I should deserve
to be hanged if I didn't!' His repeating
some parts of 'Comus' with his fine, deep,
mellow-toned voice, particularly the lines,
'I have heard my mother Circe with the
Sirens three,' &c., and the enthusiastic
comments he made afterwards, were a feast
to the ear and to the soul. He read the
poetry of Milton with the same fervour and
spirit of devotion that I have since heard
others read their own. 'That is the most
delicious feeling of all,' I have heard him
exclaim, 'to like what is excellent, no
matter whose it is.' In this respect he
practised what he preached. He was incapable of harbouring a sinister motive,

B

and judged only from what he felt. There
was no flaw or mist in the clear mirror of
his mind. He was as open to impressions
as he was strenuous in maintaining them.
He did not care a rush whether a writer
was old or new, in prose or in verse—
'What he wanted,' he said, 'was something
to make him think.' Most men's minds
are to me like musical instruments out of
tune. Touch a particular key, and it jars
and makes harsh discord with your own.
They like 'Gil Blas,' but can see nothing
to laugh at in 'Don Quixote'; they adore
Richardson, but are disgusted with Fielding. Fawcett had a taste accommodated
to all these. He was not exceptious. He
gave a cordial welcome to all sorts, pro-
vided that they were the best in their kind.
He was not fond of counterfeits or dupli-
cates. . . . His character was frank and
ingenuous in the extreme. . , . A heartier
friend or honester critic I never coped
withal."

There you have the Aristotelian χαρίεις in
the library—the ideal consumer of literary
art. He is "not exceptious" but catholic,

with " a masterly perception of all styles and
of every kind and degree of excellence." His
mind is " a clear mirror." He is open to impressions, and strenuous in maintaining them
—a lively receptivity, as we say, and a strong
enthusiasm—" wax to receive and marble
to retain." And now the question arises,
Where precisely is such a one, or the closest
approximation to such a one, to be found in
the playhouse ? Very diverse answers to
this question have been given by more or
less interested parties. According to a
familiar, though apocryphal story, Molière
sought his ideal consumer of drama in his
cook. For him ὁ χαρίεις resided in the
kitchen. A popular American actor-
manager, Mr. William Gillette, who as
the impersonator of Sherlock Holmes
ought to be infallible at detective work,
has identified ὁ χαρίεις with the man in the
street. The only critic, he says, whose
opinion he respects is the average spectator.
For Tolstoy, on the other hand, the ideal
consumer of art is the *moujik*—" a respected,
wise, educated country labourer," he says
(in his " What is Art ? ")—" one, for in-

stance, of those wise and truly religious
men whom I know among the peasants."
And, again, you have Mr. Augustine
Birrell urging the claim of the cultivated
amateur: "I have had some experience
of authors, and have always found them
better pleased with the 'unprofessional'
verdicts of educated men actively engaged
in the work of the world than ever they
were with the laboured praise of the so-
called 'expert.'" There are yet other
people who maintain that the ideal consumer of any art is the producer of it;
that the proper critic of drama is the
dramatist, of acting is the actor. I think
these various suggestions pretty well ex-
haust our possible range of choice, and it
will perhaps clear up our ideas if we
examine them in turn.

First of all, then, there is the average
spectator, the man in the pit, representing
the typical mind and taste of the crowd.
The crowd must always be mentioned first,
*honoris causâ*, in any discussion touching
the drama, because it is to an assembled
crowd that the drama is addressed. That

is the peculiarity which makes drama what
it is and not something else, not a novel or
an essay or a meditation or a fragment of
history or an exercise in pure dialectic.
And we must deal respectfully with the
playhouse crowd, because it is nothing less
than the British nation, or, to speak by
the card, that respectable minority of the
British nation which goes to the play. We
must beware of committing what J. R.
Green said was Froude's great fault, that
in a history of England he had omitted the
English people.

At the same time, the English crowd is *a*
crowd, and we have to consider for the
moment the mind of the crowd in general,
of the crowd as a crowd. The great point
about the crowd—by which I mean any
body of men and women assembled together
for a common purpose—is that it has a
mind and character of its own which differ
from the mind and character of its individual members. Collective psychology,
as the phrase goes, has only of late years
seriously engaged the attention of scientific
inquirers. A little band of Frenchmen,

headed by Professor Tarde of Paris, have taken up this study, with results which, interesting though they are, it would be here out of place to describe at length.

And so I must ask you to be good enough to take it for granted that a crowd forms a new entity, with a mind and character of its own ; that it differs from the individuals composing it just as our bodies are unlike the cells of which they are made up, or just as a chemical combination is unlike its separate ingredients. The reason, very roughly stated, is, perhaps, this. The qualities in which the members of a crowd differ from one another disappear, are mutually cancelled, while the qualities which they have in common are intensified by contact. The qualities in which men differ are principally, of course, the conscious elements of character, the fruit of education, of varying hereditary conditions, and the intelligence. The qualities, on the other hand, in which they resemble one another are principally the unconscious or subconscious qualities, the primary instincts, feelings, and passions of the race.   It follows that to bring people together in a crowd is to diminish their intellectual and to increase their emotional energy.   And so when Thackeray talked of " that great baby, the public," he was really touching a scientific truth.   The crowd has the credulity, the absence of judicial faculty, the uncontrolled violence of feeling of a child.   Shakespeare knew this when he drew the crowd in *Julius Cæsar ;* Ibsen also, when he drew the crowd in *An Enemy of Society ;* yes, and in another way, Mr. Gilbert knew it too, when he drew his little crowd of " Twelve good men and true " in *Trial by Jury.*   And this general truth is true in particular of the theatrical crowd.   The theatrical crowd is not philosophic ;  it cannot adopt a detached, impersonal, disinterested view of life ;  it must take sides.   Hence the stage convention of the " sympathetic personage." The theatrical crowd has not the judicial faculty, is not accustomed to sift evidence or to estimate probabilities.   Hence the convention of " The long arm of coincidence," and another convention—at least as old as Sophocles — that any, the wildest improbability, may be taken for the postulate, the starting - point of a play. When Œdipus the King comes on the stage he has been married for twelve years to his own mother, and throughout all that time she has never had a talk with him on the past which gives him any suspicion of who she is or of the fact that he has slain his own father. A crowd *as* a crowd is virtuous and generous ; for we are all on our best behaviour in public. Hear the gallery at a theatre of melodrama hiss the villain ! Yet it is fairly long odds that some of them have robbed their employers, and that others will go home to beat their wives. And the crowd insists upon a strict separation of virtue and vice. It wants its personages all of a piece. The composite characters, the strange blend of good and evil in all of us, it refuses to recognise. Hence the convention of " hero " and " traitor," of "immaculate heroine " and " viperine adventuress," of " poetic justice," and of " living happy ever afterwards."

You conclude that by the mere fact of forming part of an organised crowd a man descends several rungs in the ladder of civilisation. Isolated, he may be a harmless citizen, a placid British vestryman; in a crowd he becomes a barbarian, a Berserker; he "throws back" to his early ancestors. Note the effect on the theatre. "It is only the life of violence," says Maeterlinck, "the life of bygone days, that is perceived by nearly all our tragic writers; and truly one may say that anachronism dominates the stage, and that dramatic art dates back as many years as the art of sculpture. . . . To the tragic author it is only the violence of the anecdote that appeals. . . . And he imagines, forsooth, that we shall delight in witnessing the very same acts that brought joy to the hearts of the barbarians, with whom murder, outrage, and treachery were matters of daily occurrence. Whereas, it is far away from bloodshed, battle-cry, and sword-thrust that the lives of most of us flow on, and men's tears are silent to-day, and invisible and almost

spiritual. . . . Indeed, when I go to a
theatre I feel as though I were spending
a few hours with my ancestors, who con-
ceived life as something that was primitive,
arid, and brutal ; but this conception of
theirs scarcely even lingers in my memory,
and surely it is not one that I can share.
I am shown a deceived husband killing
his wife, a woman poisoning her lover, a
son avenging his father, a father slaughter-
ing his children, children putting their
father to death, murdered kings, ravished
virgins, imprisoned citizens—in a word, all
the sublimity of tradition, but, alas, how
superficial and material! Blood, surface-
tears, and death ! ”

All this, I think you will admit, takes
us very far from ὁ χαρίεις. The collective
mind, the mind of the crowd, approxi-
mates rather to the mind of primitive
man.

Further, it is peculiarly apt to be an
inattentive mind. A contributor to one
of the monthly reviews[1] has maintained

[1] Mrs. Aria in the *Nineteenth Century and After*, July
1902.

that "half the people in the theatre do
not listen to the play ; they do not go to
the theatre for that purpose, and it is
almost impossible to persuade them to do
so. They go there for some extraneous
reason far removed from a desire to follow
what is proceeding on the stage, and they
give their attention either not at all, or
in the most perfunctory fashion."

Allowing for a slight touch of exaggeration in the statement, we ought, from the
considerations I have been submitting to
you, to succeed in accounting for what
remains of truth in it. A crowd, having
an individuality of its own, cannot but
be interested in that individuality, apart
from all reference to the cause which has
brought it together. The crowd finds itself an interesting spectacle. From the
moment of its formation it becomes self-
conscious, self-assertive. To absorb its
attention—that is to say, to make it forget its own existence — is an extremely
difficult feat. How many platform orators,
how many speakers in the House of Com-
mons, how many preachers, how many

actors, can do this? So few in any generation that the whole generation knows their names. In his preface to *Le Fils Naturel* the younger Dumas compared the theatre in this respect with the church. "Like the church," he said, "we dramatists address ourselves to men assembled together, and you cannot gain the ear of the multitude for any length of time or in any efficacious way save in the name of their higher interests." The "inattention," then, of the crowd is proof of the independence and the potency of its existence. It is not really inattentive; on the contrary its attention is of the keenest, but it is directed to itself. Hence the perpetual difficulty of all arts which, like the art of the theatre, involve the presence of a crowd. The crowd has assembled because it is interested in the particular art, but, once assembled, it finds another subject of interest and a dangerous rival to the artistic subject—namely, itself.

We might perhaps find an additional reason for the inattention of the theatrical

crowd in the temperament of the typical
playgoer. Clearly, your typical playgoer
is not a reading man, a cloistered student,
a "solitary," as our forefathers used to say.
He belongs, *ex hypothesi*, to the class which
is "fond of company"; he would not, even
if he could, imitate Macaulay by reading
Plato with his feet on the fender; he must
have bustle, the sense of human kinship
brought home to him by sitting elbow to
elbow with his neighbour; he desires to see
and be seen. The faculty of intellectual
attention is seldom high in such a temperament as this. Moreover, the large majority
of a modern theatrical audience consists of
women; and it is accurate, I am afraid, if
ungallant, to say that women are the less
attentive sex. Schoolmasters who have
taken "mixed classes" tell us that it is
harder to fix the attention of their girls
than of their boys. The proof of this in
the theatre is that the parts of the house
where the women outnumber the men—
the stalls, boxes, and circle—are notoriously
less attentive than the pit and gallery, where
the men outnumber the women. Nor must

we forget that ladies in public have something else to do than merely to attend. They are on parade, they constitute a show in themselves—very often a more charming show than anything offered on the other side of the footlights.   You must frequently have been seated behind a *matinée* hat which was better worth looking at than the play of which it allowed an occasional glimpse. The argument, then, comes to this : first, that all crowds, because they are crowds, are inattentive—or, more properly speaking, self-attentive—a fact which constitutes a formidable difficulty for all arts which depend upon the crowd ; secondly, that the theatrical crowd is peculiarly inattentive, because it is drawn from the classes whose power of attention is naturally low. . . . And you perceive that we are getting further and further from ὁ χαρίεις.

But when you have fixed the attention of the crowd, how does that attention work ? The mental state of the theatrical audience, as Coleridge has pointed out, closely resembles that of a man in a dream.   In a dream you live an imaginary life as though

it were real, and yet all the time you have
a sub-consciousness that it is not real, you
know vaguely all the time that you are
only dreaming.   So, says Coleridge, "Stage-
presentations are to produce a sort of
temporary half-faith, which the spectator
encourages in himself and supports by a
voluntary contribution on his own part,
because he knows that it is at all times in
his power to see the thing as it really is.
Thus the true stage-illusion as to a forest
scene consists—not in the mind's judging it
to be a forest, but in its remission of the
judgment that it is not a forest." The
mental state, in fact, is half-way between
two extremes, absolute non-illusion and
complete delusion.

Of the first of these extremes you may
take an illustration from Tolstoy's account
of a visit to *Siegfried*.  "When I arrived,"
he says, "an actor sat on the stage amid
decorations intended to represent a cave,
and which, as is always the case, produced
the less illusion the better they were con-
structed.  He was dressed in woven tights,
with a cloak of skins, wore a wig and an

artificial beard, and with white, weak,
genteel hands (his easy movements, and
especially the shape of his stomach and his
lack of muscle, revealed the actor) beat an
impossible sword with an unnatural hammer
in a way in which no one ever uses a
hammer; and at the same time opening his
mouth in a strange way, he sang something incomprehensible." There you have
absolute non-illusion: an unsympathetic
detachment of the spectator's mind. And
now, for the other extreme state of mind,
consider some passages from Addison's
account of Sir Roger de Coverley's behaviour at a performance of *The Distrest
Mother*. "Upon the entering of Pyrrhus,
the Knight told me," says Addison, "that
he did not believe the King of France
himself had a better strut. I was indeed
very attentive to my old friend's remarks,
because I looked upon them as a piece of
natural criticism, and was well pleased to
hear him at the conclusion of almost every
scene telling me that he could not imagine
how the play would end. One while he
appeared much concerned for Andromache,

and a little while after as much for Hermione ; and was extremely puzzled to think
what would become of Pyrrhus. . . .

"When Sir Roger saw Andromache's
obstinate refusal to her Lover's impor-
tunities, he whisper'd me in the Ear, that
he was sure she would never have him ;
to which he added, with a more than
ordinary vehemence, 'You can't imagine,
Sir, what 'tis to have to do with a Widow.'
Upon Pyrrhus his threatening afterwards
to leave her, the Knight shook his Head,
and muttered to himself, 'Ay, do if you
can.' This part dwelt so much upon my
friend's imagination, that at the close of
the Third Act, as I was thinking of something else, he whispered in my Ear, 'These
widows, Sir, are the most perverse Creatures
in the World.' . . . Upon Hermione's going
off with a Menace to Pyrrhus, the Audience
gave a loud Clap; to which Sir Roger
added, 'On my word, a notable young
Baggage!'" There you have complete delusion : wholly sympathetic absorption of
the spectator's mind.

The mind of the crowd, of the average

C

spectator, is, as we have seen, somewhere between these two extremes. Now what is the state of mind of the ideal spectator, of ὁ χαρίεις? It is a rather complicated state, a state of double consciousness. There is a French proverb which says that you cannot at once join in a procession and look out of the window. Yet it is a feat of that kind which the ideal theatrical spectator has to accomplish, for remember that he is not only taking in pleasure with a complete self-surrender, he is also commanding himself so as to estimate the quality of his pleasure—while it is coming in. He must have a mental detachment as absolute as Tolstoy's at *Siegfried*—but, unlike Tolstoy's, it must be sympathetic detachment—with a sympathy as whole-hearted as Sir Roger's at *The Distrest Mother*. This by no means easy mental process requires not only an effort of the will, a special motive, but training and special aptitude. It is out of the question to look for this from the crowd.

Ὁ χαρίεις, then, the ideal spectator at the

play is not the crowd, is not the average spectator, whether Molière's cook — even though Molière's cook was that superior article a French cook—or Tolstoy's Russian peasant, or the man who naïvely asks if dramatic critics are of any use.

After the crowd, the average or uncultivated amateur, let us turn to Mr. Birrell's candidate for the critical post—the man of affairs or of the world who dabbles in the arts ; in other words, the amateur of culture. Mr. Birrell puts in a very artful plea for this class. He says the authors like them, preferring their "verdicts of approval" to the "laboured praise of the so-called 'expert.'" Here, however, we must be on our guard against the rhetorical device of the professional advocate—the familiar device of comparing one thing at its best with another thing at its worst. The praise of the "expert" is not necessarily "laboured." And you will observe that the authors like the men of the world when they deliver "verdicts of approval." What the authors think of this class when they deliver verdicts of disapproval we are not told.

However, I willingly admit there is something very seductive in the idea of every cultivated gentleman being his own critic—though there is a little treatise called " Every man his own lawyer," which Mr. Birrell, I expect, regards with some suspicion. Criticism from that point of view is very much like the game of golf —which is said to be as good for the duffer as for the expert, and especially good for the middle-aged and even elderly. It is a notion which particularly recommends itself to us English — who are governed by amateurs. That, in fact, is part and parcel of the British Constitution. Small wonder, then, that we should take as quite a natural thing the *obiter dicta* of the amateur in the comparatively humble region of the arts. But here I think we must distinguish. It would be inaccurate, as well as impertinent, to label the critical writings or discourses of such men as Mr. Gladstone or Mr. Balfour or Lord Rosebery —names which at once occur to everybody's mind in this connection—as amateurish. Whatever else they were or are, these men were or are men of letters,

serious students of their subject. When
we refer to the amateur of culture, we are
thinking of a class opposed to the literary
class, the mundane people, a class which
has not the patience or the leisure or the
aptitude for serious study of the arts, their
history, their laws, their logic, a class to
which the arts are a pastime, and nothing
but a pastime. Now the criticism of these
mundane people is always worth listening
to, just as is the criticism of the man in the
street. For it is a criticism which is, at
any rate, free from the literary bias, from
the cant of criticism, from the smell of the
lamp. It seldom fails to give us a fresh and
suggestive view of the subject. But does it
give us the right view? I am afraid not.
For though it is free from the literary, the
professional bias, it has a bias of its own—
which is either the bias of the individual or
the bias of the mode. As for the bias of
the individual, you get that in the men of
autocratic temper — who take their own
subjective opinions for the measure of
universal truth. This bias is illustrated
by Lord Foppington in *The Relapse*, who

preferred the "natural sprouts" of his own
brain to the "forced products" of another
man's. This bias is also illustrated by the
opinions of George II. on "bainting and
boetry," of George III. on "that sad stuff,
Shakespeare," of Frederick the Great on
epic poetry, which, he declared, reached its
highest pinnacle in Voltaire's "Henriade,"
and by the opinions of an illustrious successor of Frederick's on every art under the
sun. It is perhaps permissible to suggest
that the artistic views of that illustrious
monarch, interesting and instructive as they
are to the historian and the student of
character, are not exactly the opinions of
the Aristotelian χαρίεις. Then as to the
bias of the mode, everybody knows how
fashion rules the mundane amateur —
fashion, the most changeable, the most
relative to time and place, the least reason-
able thing in the world. At one time
the mundane amateur is all for "Grecian
marbles," at another he is all for the
paintings of Domenichino or Sir Thomas
Lawrence. To be sure fashion sometimes
makes a good shot: Garrick became the

fashion at once. But it is at haphaz-
ard. The fashionable people, the mundane
amateurs, who made the vogue of Kean,
also made the vogue of Master Betty.
There are no settled principles of judgment
here.

And there is another subdivision of
the cultivated amateur, not the mundane
sort, but the intellectual sort—no doubt
the sort which Mr. Birrell has in mind
—which is quite as unfitted to run a
successful candidate for the post of ideal
spectator. " Probably there is nothing,"
said the late Mr. Grant Allen, "which
serious intellects hate so much as an intellectual treat! To be made to sit out a
performance at the Français or the Lyceum
would be to a great many of us an unmitigated bore. I believe high-class music,
high - class plays, high - class novels are
produced mainly for people of moderate or
medium intelligence ; people whose brains
and bodies are systematically underworked.
Men who have done a good day's toil with
head or hands don't care for *Faust :* they
want a Gaiety burlesque. The silliest

song, the most rollicking fun, of the Café Chantants in the Champs Elysées or of the London Pavilion, is to many intelligent men a far greater relaxation than the best-mounted piece of Shakespeare's or Victor Hugo's. Or rather, the one is a relaxation and the other a nuisance." Well, we can all understand that point of view, and, in certain moods, sympathise with it ; but at the same time we can all see that it is not the point of view of the ideal spectator, of ὁ χαρίεις at the play.

And now we have done with the amateur, whether of the street or of the *salon*, whether intellectual or mundane, and must look for our ideal spectator in quite another quarter. It is often said that the ideal consumer of drama, or of any other art, is the producer of it. The proper judges, that is, of pictures are painters, of novels are novelists, of plays are playwrights, and of acting are actors.

> " Let such teach others who themselves excel,
> And censure others who have written well,"

says Pope in his "Essay on Criticism." This is a very plausible contention, which

has hoodwinked many worthy people.   For
here, also, we have a notion which reflects
the English spirit: trial by jury, judgment
by our peers.   And if criticism were a
mode of technical instruction, a piece of
didactic, the contention would, no doubt,
be a perfectly sound one.   I will go further
and insist that, whenever we say that this
or that play is bad, this or that picture
ill-painted, this or that symphony poorly
orchestrated, we ought always to bear in
mind the difficulties of the artist's task and
to remember that these things which he
has failed to do well we, very likely, cannot do at all.   That is a chastening reflec-
tion, a salutary moral exercise; but though
it may prompt us to charity, it ought not to
affect our ultimate verdict.   John Dennis
effectively answered Pope that his precept
"is denied by matter of fact, and by the
experience of above two thousand years."[1]
On this point, as on so many others, we
get something decisive from the strong
common-sense of Samuel Johnson.   Boswell

[1] " Reflections upon a late Rhapsody call'd, An Essay upon
Criticism ; by Mr. Dennis."

had collaborated with two other friends in writing a pamphlet entitled " Critical Strictures " against Mallet's tragedy of *Elvira ;* but one of the friends had misgivings, and said, " We have hardly a right to abuse this tragedy : for bad as it is, how vain should either of us be to write one not near so good." Then Johnson broke in, " Why, no, sir ; this is not just reasoning. You may abuse a tragedy, though you cannot write one. You may scold a carpenter who has made you a bad table, though you cannot make a table. It is not your trade to make tables." [1]

So it is not the dramatic critic's trade to make plays, or to teach the way to make plays. It is the function of criticism not to inculcate methods, but to appraise results ; to examine the thing done, not the way to do it. It is, in short, the evaluation of pleasurable impressions ; and to receive these impressions, we must have a perfectly open mind—a clear mirror, as Hazlitt said of Joseph Fawcett. Now your actual, your so-called " creative," artist is too narrow

[1] Dr. Birbeck Hill's edition of Boswell, vol. i. p. 409.

and too intense for that. The very force within him which gives the impulse to creation is fatal to catholicity of taste. His "personal equation," as the astronomers call it, will not permit him to be an accurate observer. Every critical preference he expresses is really a veiled justification of himself. As Stendhal said, every eulogy between *confrère* and *confrère* is a certificate of resemblance. Of this you will find an amusing instance in Aubrey de Vere's Reminiscences of Tennyson in early days:

"'Read the exquisite songs of Burns,' Tennyson exclaimed. 'In shape, each of them has the perfection of the berry, in light the radiance of the dew-drop: you forget for its sake those stupid things, his serious pieces.' The same day," continues Aubrey de Vere, "I met Wordsworth and named Burns to *him*. Wordsworth praised him even more vehemently than Tennyson had done; but added, 'Of course I refer to his serious efforts; those foolish little amatory songs of his one has to forget.' I told the tale to Henry Taylor the same evening, and his answer was: 'Burns' exquisite songs and Burns' serious efforts are to me alike tedious and disagreeable reading.'"

These are authors when they praise, but when they don't! You know what Corneille thought of Racine; what Richardson thought of Fielding and what Fielding of Richardson; what Borrow and Peacock, two very different authors, agreed in thinking about a third author, Walter Scott; what Byron said of Keats; what Macready thought of Charles Kean and Charles Kean of Macready; what Beaconsfield said of Thackeray, and Charlotte Brontë of Jane Austen.

And then there is the trite but inevitable remark, that the nature which invents and combines — the faculty of the socalled " creative " artist—is widely different —though I hope to persuade you later that it is by no means totally different—from the nature which enjoys and analyses—the critical faculty. But there is really no need to argue the point. It was settled, once and for all, by the excellent, the invaluable Aristotle, in Book III. ch. ii. of his " Poli-

tics," where you may read: "Thus it is
not the builder alone whose function it is
to criticise the merits of a house; the
person who uses it, to wit, the householder,
is actually a better judge; and, similarly, a
pilot is a better judge of a helm than a
carpenter; or one of the company of a
dinner than the cook."

# II

## THE DRAMATIC CRITIC

## II

THE way ought now to be clear for a consideration of the expert playgoer, the so-called dramatic critic. I have pointed out that we are all critics in a sense—criticism being the reaction of mind against mind, the opinion of the consumer about the work of art which the producer offers him—and I have postulated, after Aristotle, and indeed not only after Aristotle, but in accordance with common-sense and the nature of things, an ideal consumer, the man of the perfect taste and the right opinion, whom Aristotle calls ὁ χαρίεις. We have examined how far and in what way the several classes among consumers of drama diverged from this standard, the ideal consumer. There is the representative of the crowd, with the marked limitations imposed by the mental conditions peculiar to crowds. There is the cultivated

D

amateur, whether mundane or intellectual,
with his limitations, which, for the mundane amateur, are the caprice of fashion
in artistic taste, and the fact that art is
for him only a pastime, just as it is only a
pastime, a rest from brain-fag, for a certain
sort of intellectual amateur. We have
scrutinised the claims of the producer himself, the playwright or the actor, to be the
nearest approximation to the Aristotelian
χαρίεις in the theatre, and we have rejected
the claims of the producer because his own
special artistic individuality is of necessity
so strong as to colour his general ideas,
and to disqualify him from forming a broad
and balanced judgment. Still, these classes
are all critics in their way. They are *vivâ
voce* critics; and they are irresponsible
critics, caring not a rush for antiquity or
posterity, or for anything beyond their
pleasure of the moment. And remember
that this floating mass of irresponsible *vivâ
voce* criticism is enormously important to
the producers of art; for, one way or
another, it is the criticism which settles
their hash. Authors complain of the se-

verity or captiousness, or even malice, of
what is written about them by the re-
sponsible "official" critics; but if they
only heard what is said about them by
the irresponsible *vivâ voce* critics!

We come now, then, to the class of
critics properly so called, who differ from
all these other classes in that it is their
business not only, like the others, to enjoy,
but to appraise and to justify their enjoy-
ment. And this appraising and justification have to be made systematic and to
be presented in literary form. Hence the
critics proper are in the peculiar position
of being at once consumers and producers;
they are consumers of one art, the art of
drama, and producers of another art, the
art of criticism. In other words, the critic
has something more to do than to approxi-
mate as closely as may be to the ideal
spectator — though that to be sure is a
very important, perhaps the fundamental,
part of his task—he has, over and above
that, to be an artist. This claim of criticism to be an art is viewed with some
jealousy by other artists, who are fond of

making the distinction that their arts—the poem, the novel, the play—are "creative" arts, whereas criticism is not "creation." This distinction, I cannot but think, is shallow and lamentably unscientific. Science teaches us that there is no such thing as creation; only change, transmutation. But accepting the word "creation," we must apply it to all producers of literary art, whether they be poets or novelists or playwrights or critics. They are all creators, and what they all create is æsthetic feeling. And the raw material out of which they all create this is the same, namely, themselves. Criticism, like any other art —whatever else it may be—is a mode of self-expression. M. Anatole France has given a famous description of criticism as "The adventures of a soul among masterpieces," and he has added: "In order to be frank, the critic ought to say; Gentlemen, I am about to speak of myself *à propos* of Shakespeare, or Racine, or Pascal, or Goethe — by no means a bad opportunity." Let us have done, then, with this false old criterion of "creation" as a pretext for giving the name of art to the Adventures of Robinson Crusoe or of Harry Richmond, and withholding it from the Adventures of a Soul among Master-pieces.

To see what nonsense this criterion really is, you need only take the case of Dry-den. Are we seriously to be told that while Dryden in his *Wild Gallant,* or in his *All for Love,* or in his *Spanish Friar* was doing creative work, he was not, for-sooth, doing creative work in his *Essay of Dramatic Poesy?* Why, the very scheme of this beautiful piece, the contrast of a pure classic gem against a rich romantic setting, is, in itself, a creation. " It was that memorable day, in the first summer of the late war, when our navy engaged the Dutch; a day wherein the two most mighty and best appointed fleets which any age had ever seen, disputed the command of the greater half of the globe, the com-merce of nations, and the riches of the universe. . . . The noise of the cannons from both navies reached our ears about the City, so that all men being alarmed with it, and in a dreadful suspense of the event which we knew was then deciding, every one went following the sound as his fancy led him ; . . . all seeking the noise in the depths of silence." . . . And so four gentlemen in long perruques, magnificent creatures, took a barge and waited to begin talking until the rush of waters under London Bridge was out of their ears and, getting towards Greenwich, they could order the watermen to let fall their oars more gently. And what could these courtly gentlemen find better to talk about than dramatic criticism? What the drama is, and was, and may some day be, and what are the Three Unities, and whether rhyme or blank verse is better for tragedy, and whether the Ancients surpass the Moderns and the French the English, and what is to be thought of Terence his plots and of Shakespeare and Beaumont and Fletcher and Ben Jonson. And, then, how artfully the plot of this critical drama is related to the scenic background, so that the very swallows which skim the water ahead of the barge are pressed into service to give

a simile for the literary points of some
poet under discussion! And by-and-by
the watermen are bidden to turn the barge
and row softly, that the party may take
the cool of the evening in their return;
and the talk flows on, as abundant and
as richly laden as the river itself, and the
boom of the Dutch guns has now given
place to the serene wisdom of Aristotle—
the thought of whom among those peri-
wigs suggests a Grecian marble over against
a Sir Peter Lely. And so rapt were these
gentlemen in their discourse that it was
not until they had been twice or thrice
called to, that they saw the barge had
stopped, and they were back at the foot
of Somerset stairs. And then there is the
choice little final kinematograph:—" The
company stood a-while looking back on
the water, which the moonbeams played
upon, and made it appear like floating
quick-silver; at last they went up through
a crowd of French people, who were merrily
dancing in the open air, and nothing concerned for the noise of guns which had
alarmed the town that afternoon."

What an exquisite blend of frank " impressionism " and academic theory, of the circumstance of the moment and the eternal verities, of Pepysian London and the Athens of the greater Peripatetic! It is because of the special quality of this blend, its peculiar " thrill "—the Hellenisation, so to speak, of a London day—that I cannot resist the temptation of setting beside this Essay of Dryden's a passage from one of Edward FitzGerald's Letters, where he describes to a friend a jaunt he had in town with James Spedding, the learned editor of Bacon :—

"The most pleasurable remembrance I had of my stay in town," writes FitzGerald, " was the last day I spent there, having a long ramble in the streets with Spedding, looking at books and pictures; then a walk with him and Carlyle across the Park to Chelsea, where we dropped that Latter Day Prophet at his house; then, getting upon a steamer, smoked down to Westminster; dined at a chop-house by the Bridge, and then went to Astley's; old Spedding being quite as wise about the

Horsemanship as about Bacon and Shakespeare.   We parted at midnight in Covent-
Garden; and this whole pleasant day has
left a taste on my palate like one of
Plato's lighter, easier, and more picturesque
dialogues."

It is when we come to recognise that
the critic is himself an artist, in his way,
that we see the full extent of fatuity
in the question, "What is the *use* of
Dramatic Criticism?" The use of any
art is as a channel for the communi-
cation of ideas and emotions between
man and man.   It is a mode by which
the producer of the art shares out his
moods, his soul-states, his views of life,
with the consumer.   This is what is
meant in popular language by "being
interesting."   Just as you may have an interesting novel or an interesting play, so
you may have an "interesting" dramatic
criticism.   And that is the use of it.

Well, the peculiar position, the *differentia*, of the critic proper results from
the fact that he has to be not only
consumer but producer, not only observer

but artist.    It is that which chiefly dis-
tinguishes him from the other critics
whom we have passed in review—from
the man in the street, the connoisseur,
and the rest of them—in a word, from
the public.  Not that his attitude, merely
as an observer, a consumer, is quite the
same as theirs.  We have noted the con-
tagious influence of the crowd and its
results.  Now, just as the able theatre-
manager is he who allows for that con-
tagious influence, is indeed a kind of
professional incendiary, always watching
when he can set the crowd on fire, so
the critic is the one man in the theatre
whose business it is to react against the
crowd, to " sit tight," as the phrase goes,
and to preserve the independence of his
personal judgment, the captaincy of his
soul.  He has to be on his guard, too,
against those caprices of literary fashion
which sway the mundane amateur, and,
on the other hand, against that professional bias which influences the actual
producer of drama, be he playwright or
player.  But, as I say, the main dif-

ference between the critic proper and the public at large is the consequence of the peculiar position of the critic as being himself an artist.

This disagreement between critics and public is a subject which nobody seems to be in danger of forgetting. Whenever an instance of it occurs the critics' good-natured friends—they have many at such moments — sedulously improve the occasion. " Well, you see you were wrong in ' slating ' So-and-so's piece ; the advertisements already announce its hundredth night." Or, " What on earth did you mean by praising that rubbish at the Frivolity ? Why, it didn't run a week ! " The genial implication in either case is that the critic has been an ass for his pains. But any one who has ever thought the matter over knows that talk of this kind is nothing to the purpose. Take, for an historic instance, the disagreement between critics and public in mid-eighteenth century. While English critics of the Chesterfield type were learning to praise French " regularity," a French critic

like Diderot could wax enthusiastic over
the "irregular, rugged, and wild air of
the English genius." But there was no
mutual concession of this kind on the
part of the two publics. Between the
critical and the public attitude Mrs.
Centlivre (in her preface to *Love's Con-
trivance*) had already made a practical distinction :—

"The critics cavil most about decorums,
and cry up Aristotle's rules, as the most
essential part of the play. I own they
are in the right of it ; yet I dare venture
they'll never persuade the town to be of
their opinion."

The plain truth is that the playgoer
who is merely seeking his pleasure and
the playgoer who has to appraise and to
justify his pleasure of necessity take somewhat different views. For the one there
is the sole question, Am I pleased ? For
the other there is that question too,
but coupled with another question — a
question which, by the way, was one of
Matthew Arnold's many borrowings from
Sainte-Beuve—Am I right to be pleased ?

Stendhal's precept, "Interroge-toi quand tu ris," is nothing to the public, but it is everything to the critic. Or the public may say, "we were bored," and forget the play as quickly as they can. The critics have to say why they are bored, and that is a bore, so that they are sure to be less charitable to a bad play than the public. The wound is kept open. Then it has to be remembered that good plays, plays which rightly please the public, often make bad "copy"—that is to say, unworkable material — for the critic. A play that presents no variation of type may be interesting enough in itself, but vexes the critic, to whom it offers no "purchase." And, to go a little further into technical particulars, there are certain classes of play—for example, melodramas and farces—which always come out worse on paper than on the boards. The critic is generally tempted to describe melodrama by the ironic method—which is a perfidy —and to narrate the plot of a farce is, at the best, to decant champagne. It is for a kindred reason that the "drama of ideas" is apt to be overpraised in print—which is a good medium for ideas. In brief, criticism, being a form of literature, can do justice to the literary elements in drama ; but in drama there are many other elements, and criticism is often at fault with these, because of a purely technical difficulty, the difficulty of transposing the effects of one art into the effects of another. Criticism can give the reader a very fair idea of *Hamlet* or *Paolo and Francesca*, of *Le Demi-Monde* or *A Doll's House*, of *Iris* or *The Admirable Crichton*. It can give only an inadequate account of the pleasure afforded by *A Midsummer Night's Dream* or *La Locandiera* or *L'Enfant Prodigue*. With *Box and Cox* or *Charley's Aunt* it can do nothing.

And we have seen the reason why. It is because the critic, like the piece of furniture in Goldsmith's poem, has "a double debt to pay"; because he is at once consumer and producer, at once parasite and independent, substantive artist. In the very act of describing and appraising the methods of another art he has to follow the methods,

the very different methods, of his own.   A
criticism is a picture with its own laws of
perspective and composition and "values,"
and the play which furnishes the subject for
this picture has more often than not to
be "humoured" a little, stretched here and
squeezed there, in order to fit into the
design.   The salient points in the pattern
of the play may not suit the salient points
in the pattern of the criticism—though, no
doubt, the good critic is he who most often
gets the two sets into perfect coincidence.
The critic must have his "general idea,"
his leading theme, which gives his criticism
its unity, something to hold it together.
This general idea, however legitimately it
may have been derived from the play
criticised, will very likely get exaggerated,
will assume a much more important part
in the criticism than it actually did in the
play itself.   Or the critic may take some
significant phrase or catchword of the play
as a "refrain" for his article, or he may
perform a *fantasia* on some leading theme
of the play (for example, the "nose" theme
in *Cyrano de Bergerac*), until he has ex-

hausted all its possible permutations and combinations. These are devices permissible in criticism, because criticism is literature, an art intended to interest, to give pleasure, in itself; but their effect is to warp the genuine first-hand impression of the play, to alter its proportions. Thus criticism tends to systematise what may not be systematic, to follow out its own logic and to expand its own formulas, rather than to conform strictly to the outline and proportions of the thing criticised. That is so, because, in a sense, all art is not only a transformation but a deformation of its subject-matter. It is the old difficulty of the portrait painter. The sitter asks, " Is it like ? " ; the connoisseur, " Is it a good piece of painting ? " There are whole elements of a play which are ignored by the critic, for the simple reason that they will not work into his scheme. One has even heard of cases where the name of some meritorious actor has been passed over in silence, because mention of it would spoil the hang of the critic's sentence ; but that is immoral.

One must not be lured into betraying all the secrets of the craft. Enough has been said, perhaps, to show why the critic and the public differ in their opinions of the same thing, and why this difference is widened in the very process by which the critic records his opinions. It is often widened still further by what may seem a purely mechanical accident—the interval of time which elapses between the critic's impression and his record of it. The objection is often raised against " first night " criticism, that it is bound to be hasty, undigested, more or less of an improvisation. Apart from the fact that newspaper readers, in any case, insist upon having it, I believe that it is on the whole the criticism most advantageous to the play. The critic's sensations are vivid, his mind is full of his subject, he still has the proportions and details of the play in his eye. Writing after an interval, he is apt to remember his general impression of the play rather than the play itself, and his impression has lost in truth by the fading of minor detail, to the consequent exaggera-

E

tion of a few prominent features—a process which may lead the most conscientious critic to unconscious caricature.

Now I trust I have not been showing you a glimpse of the critic at work without at the same time suggesting to you his professional drawbacks, his besetting sins. For one thing, I have said that he has often to give an appearance of system to subject-matter which is not really systematic. And so he is apt to become what Joe Gargery would call too "architectooralooral." Then again, having to deal perpetually in formulas, he is in danger of becoming their dupe. He is apt to indulge in what another character in Dickens calls "poll-parrotting"; to repeat mechanically cant phrases —"objective" and "subjective," "classic" and "romantic," "organism" and "environment," "development" and "reaction." These are the things which Sir Leslie Stephen, with his wonted manliness and homeliness of sense, brands as "the mere banalities of criticism. I can never hear them," he says, "without a suspicion that a professor of Æsthetics is trying to hood-

wink me by a bit of technical platitude.
The cant phrases which have been used so
often by panegyrists, too lazy to define
their terms, have become almost as mean-
ingless as the complimentary formulæ of
society." And that is just it; the man of
letters is here showing the same weakness
as the man of the world. For there are
fashions in the library just as there are
fashions in the *salon;* and the desire for
imitation for imitation's sake, is common
to all humanity.

And then the critic is apt to theorise "in
the air," because of the constant tendency
towards divorce between literature and life.
Walter Bagehot makes some characteristic
remarks on this point : " The reason why
so few good books are written, is that few
people that can write know anything. In
general an author has always lived in a
room, has read books, has cultivated science,
is acquainted with the style and sentiments
of the best authors, but is out of the way
of employing his own ears and eyes. He
has nothing to hear and nothing to see.
His life is a vacuum. . . . He sits beside a

library-fire, with nice white paper, a good pen, a capital style, every means of saying everything, and nothing to say. . . . How dull it is to make it your business to write, to stay by yourself in a room to write, and then to have nothing to say." Something like that is very often the fate of the dramatic critic. For there are many plays which are absolutely null and void. The general playgoer settles the matter quite comfortably by falling asleep over them. The critic has to say something, and in reality there is nothing to be said.

So much by way of confession of critical sins. There remain two charges constantly brought against critics which may be admitted to the full, but which, instead of being to their discredit, are really the best evidence of their good faith and their good work. These two charges are : first, lack of unanimity—the critics disagree with one another—and, second, lack of consistency—the critic will often disagree with himself. Critics, it is said, not being unanimous, cannot be representative of public opinion. As though public opinion about a play was

ever unanimous !  We must not be fooled by
a noun of multitude.   " Public " is one word ;
it does not denote one thing.   I know I
spoke in my first lecture of the crowd as
a whole, and sketched the general aspects
of the collective mind.   But the public,
of course, is extraordinarily disparate in
its parts.   It comprises the people who
applaud a play, the people who hiss it, the
people who slumber through it, the people
who don't know what to think about it, the
people who like it because dear Angelina
does, the people who dislike it because they
had to forgo their after-dinner coffee in
order to see it, and the people who would
stay away from it if they were not paid
to go.   So that when criticism is unanimous,
then, and only then, shall we be able to say
confidently that it is not representative.
But fortunately that time—that monotonous
time — will never be.   For in that time
there will have to be absolute rules for
judging works of art, applied by everybody
in the same way ;  all critics will possess
the same principles, taste, temperament,
intellectual education, moral standard, and

experience of life. Meanwhile, " with such a being as man in such a world as the present "—as Bishop Butler used to phrase it—no two critics who are thinking and feeling for themselves can be in complete agreement. We might as well complain that their faces are not alike! There is, no doubt, often a certain appearance of unanimity among critics who are not thinking for themselves but are trying to think what they suppose they ought to think or what they guess other people to be thinking, so as to shout, on Mr. Pickwick's principle, with the largest crowd. But these are critics who have mistaken their vocation. So that when Mr. Sydney Grundy asks, " When critics fall out, who shall decide ? " and when Sir Henry Irving refers to " the rapture of disagreement which is served up by the dramatic critics," they ought in reality to have been gratified by the lack of unanimity which they deplore. It is evidence that the plays of the one and the acting of the other are stimulating enough to force the critics into thinking for themselves.

We have seen that while criticism as to
its substance is opinion, as to its form it is
art. No two opinions can be the same,
because no man has the same perceptive
apparatus — eye, ear, nerves, brain — as
another man. Is it not notorious that
no two people will agree in describing
the simplest fact, the pace of an omnibus,
the number of cats in the back garden?
But while criticism is bound to vary, as
mere record of fact, its variation is enormously increased because it is an art. Did
you ever see two identical pictures of the
same subject by different hands? Did you
ever hear two pianists play the same sonata
in the same way? Of course not, and yet
there are people who seem to expect different souls to have the same adventures
among the masterpieces. And if they
were the same, there would still remain
the variations of ability to describe them.
The critic's real difficulty is that he never
does describe them adequately. To adjust
language with exactness to one's thoughts
and impressions is an impossible feat;
critics, like other writers, spend their lives

in practising it, and, like other writers, never bring the feat off.

As to the critic's want of self-consistency, that is apt in this country to bring him into sad trouble. In 1902 a provincial jury mulcted a newspaper in the sum of £100 and costs for a certain theatrical "notice," and two of the jurors wrote to the newspapers to say that the main ground of their verdict was the consideration that the notice was inconsistent with a former notice of the same play in the same quarter. If these gentlemen had been philosophers— instead of jurymen—they would have congratulated this inconsistent critic on the plain proof that he was not a mechanical recording instrument—a barometer or a pair of scales—a dead thing, but a human being with the principle of growth and life within him. They would have recognised, with a pure natural joy, that the soul never has the same adventures twice over. Nothing—to take perhaps a less humble literary example—nothing could be more interesting than to note the mental development of the well-known Danish critic, Dr.

George Brandes, in studying the works of Ibsen *pari passu* with their production. He says himself, after noting how Ibsen at different stages of his work was not the same Ibsen: " But neither was his critic quite the same. He had in the meantime gone through a great deal, and had consequently acquired a larger outlook upon life, and a more flexible emotional nature. He had dropped all the doctrines that were due to education and tradition. He understood the poet better now." A great historical instance of development in the reverse direction is that of Voltaire in regard to Shakespeare. Voltaire began by blessing Shakespeare (with reservations), and ended by (quite unreservedly) cursing him. That was by no means because he understood the poet better; but for reasons extraneous to his critical development, reasons connected with his objections to the course which he found the French drama was taking without his leave. And the moral of that little affair is that the critic should remain content to be an artist, and not set up for a literary dictator.

And note this about the changes in the critic's mental experience; they only reproduce in the individual what has always been happening in the race; they are the life-history, in miniature, of the whole body of criticism. For example, it has been a persistent cry of criticism throughout the ages that the present age is witnessing the decline of drama. M. Sarcey[1] gave a long list of theatrical pamphlets bought at a collector's sale, from which I select only a few titles and dates:—

1768. Causes de la décadence du théâtre.
1771. Du théâtre et des causes de sa décadence.
1807. Les causes de la décadence du théâtre.
1828. Considérations sur les causes de la décadence du théâtre.
1841. Recherches sur les causes de la décadence du théâtre.
1842. A quelles causes attribuer la décadence de la tragédie en France?
1849. De la décadence de l'art dramatique.
1860. De la décadence des théâtres.
1866. Rapport au Sénat sur la décadence de l'art dramatique.
1871. De la décadence des théâtres.
1876. Cri d'alarme sur la situation de l'art dramatique.
1880. Du théâtre à sauver.

---

[1]. *Quarante Ans de Théâtre*, v. i. p. 185 (Paris, 1902).

Our English critical wailings, if less numerous, have been not a whit less monotonous. The following specimens are culled, almost at random, from Mr. R. W. Lowe's " Bibliographical Account of English Theatrical Literature " : [1]—

1819. A Letter on the decay and degradation of English theatrical literature.
1826. A nostrum for theatrical insipidity.
1853. A New Drama or we faint ! ! !  Decline of the Drama ! ! !
1885. The truth about the stage; "something rotten in the, etc."

Of course the perpetual cry of the drama in decline is but the other side of a perpetual change in the theatrical consumer's taste, and, in fact, new critical demands are among the oldest things in the world. Throughout the ages there is not a dramatist of them all but has recognised, at the moment of writing, a new critical demand, a demand which was to be humoured, or derided, or temporised with, or even attributed to his own prescience and invention, as the case might be. Is there not the leading instance of Shakespeare, speaking

[1] London, 1888.

through the Chorus in *Henry V.?* What
was his appeal to the audience for the freer
exercise of their imagination but a tacit
recognition of the new demand expressed
by Sidney in his "Apologie for Poetry"—
Sidney was one of our earliest dramatic
critics—the demand for a closer verisimili-
tude of the scene? And did not John
Webster, in his preface to *The White Devil*,
openly deride the new critical demand of
his age—that novelty which is a critical
demand of every age? "I have noted,"
says he, "most of the people that come to
the playhouse resemble those ignorant asses
who, visiting stationers' shops, their use is
not to inquire for good books, but new
books." So Corneille, in his preface to *Le
Cid*, temporised with the new critical demand
of his time for historical fidelity, by faking
up documentary evidence in favour of his
story; while Racine, in his preface to
*Bérénice*, defended his evasion of the new
critical demand for an ingeniously invented
plot, by citing the simple fables of Greek
tragedy. In our later times Victor Hugo
discusses the new critical demand of the

romantic movement, the demand for the
beautiful-ugly and the sublime-grotesque,
in his preface to *Cromwell;* Dumas *fils*,
in his preface to *Le Fils Naturel*, defers to
a new critical demand in vaunting his aim
of pressing the drama into the service of
great social reforms and the great hopes of
humanity; and to-day there is Mr. Bernard
Shaw, who is at once a critic and a producer
of drama, professedly writing plays to meet
a new critical demand for a drama whose
outlook upon life shall be that of a "genu-
inely scientific natural history."

Now what is the explanation of this
perpetual variation of the critical demand?
The explanation is to be found in the simple
fact that the drama, being an art, shares the
primary aim of all art, which is to give
pleasure. And this pleasure of art, it must
be borne in mind, is in the first instance—
whatever higher forms it may take in the
long run—a pleasure of the senses. It is
not the intellectual pleasure of solving a
proposition of Euclid, nor is it the moral
pleasure of letting a good deed shine in a
naughty world. A picture, whatever else

it does, must first please the eye; music,
whatever else it does, must first please the
ear.    And pleasure of the senses—this is
the important point—is only to be had at
the price of perpetual change; for it is an
elementary physiological law that the mere
repetition of the same stimulus will not be
followed by the same pleasurable reaction.
Contrast art, in this respect, with *pure*
science or with *fundamental* morals.    Pure
science does not change, and cannot, so long
as man remains as we know him.    Have
not two and two always made four, two
sides of a triangle always been greater than
the third, two bodies in space always
attracted one another inversely as the
square of the distance between them?
And, so long as man remains in society
as we know it, the first principles of conduct cannot change:—Thou shalt not kill,
steal, bear false witness against thy neighbour.    No so with art.    Our pleasure-sense
becomes sharpened by use, more subtle,
more exacting.    In order to procure the
same thrill we are driven to vary and to
intensify the exciting cause; or, as Mr.

Arthur Balfour has pithily expressed it in one of those amiable digressions with which he has enlivened his " Foundations of Belief "—he is actually speaking of music, but the statement may be generalised—" A steady level of æsthetic sensation can only be maintained by increasing doses of æsthetic stimulant." So true is this of the theatre that, to provide the same sum of pleasure for the spectator, dramatic interest has to go on multiplying its intensity, in the course of time, by something like a geometrical progression. Terence took two plays of Menander to make one of his own, and M. Brunetière computes that there are two of Terence's in one of Molière's, while to make a play of Dumas or Augier you have to add one of Molière's to one of Diderot's or Sedaine's.

But, it may be objected, if art is always transforming itself in response to this demand for a change of pleasure-stimulus, what about those works of art which we call classics ? Are they not stable and permanent ? Indeed, do we not call the very greatest classics immortal ? And the reply is, that in the existence of the classics lies the very proof of the point. For the virtue of a classic, the quality which gives it that rank, is the property of self-renewal, the property of responding in different ages to different demands for pleasure. Every generation refashions the classics for itself, extracting an entirely new pleasure out of them, so that—to take only one example— you have Aristophanes praising Homer as a moralist, as a teacher of good life, and the seventeenth century admiring Homer for his "correctness," the "nice conduct of his fable," while the twentieth century enjoys Homer for his primitive simplicity, his fairy tale romance, and his "barbaric yaup."

The history of all criticism then—and of dramatic criticism no less than any other species—is, and must be, a history of variations. But to compile a history is not our present affair. At the head of a long list of projected works—projected but never begun—which Johnson gave to his friend Langton and Langton presented to George III. (who must have been highly edified), stands a "History of Criticism,

as it relates to judging of authors, from
Aristotle to the present age.  An account
of the rise and improvements of that art ; of
the different opinions of authors, ancient and
modern."  As Johnson's whole life proved
insufficient for that adventure, one may
hope to stand excused for not attempting
a history of dramatic criticism in a brief
course of lectures.  Enough if it be found
possible within our narrow limits to glance at
this Aristotle, with whom Johnson would,
as in duty bound, have begun, and to trace
the vicissitudes through the ages of one or
two of his leading ideas.  Many of those
ideas have kept steadily travelling in the
world up to this moment—though I think
we shall find that, as Voltaire said of something else, they have become *diablement
changées en route*.  For I cannot help sus-
pecting a certain spice of exaggeration in
much current talk about the "modernity"
of Aristotle.  You have, for example, Mr.
Herbert Paul, an accomplished scholar and
a most sagacious critic, roundly declaring
that "Aristotle is of all Greeks the most
modern," and that his *Poetics* are "intensely

F

modern." But what is meant by saying that an old author is "modern"? Surely, that the "whirligig of time" has turned full circle, that the author's opportunity has come up again, through some quality of his mind or temper which makes him peculiarly at home in our own day. Thus a good deal of Montaigne may justly be called "modern" in this age of introspection and Bashkirtseffism. In the same way some of the little intimate passages in Euripides seem strangely "modern" in this age of "naturalistic" literature. But that is not the sense in which you can apply the word "modern" to Aristotle; I think we shall by-and-by encounter another Greek critic who, in that sense, was very much more "modern." Those things in Aristotle which are valid and fresh to-day are not more valid than they were in the day of Elizabeth, or than they were in the day of Louis XIV. It is, for such things, a case of the eternal verities, not the case of Sir Roger de Coverley's coat, which had been in and out of the fashion a dozen times. Euclid is true to-day, but he is not accurately to

be described as "intensely modern." And
mention of Euclid recalls the other mistake
which has been persistently made in dealing
with Aristotle: the reverencing of all his
leading ideas as though they were even
something more than eternal verities, as
though they were holy sacraments. Thus
to Lessing he was as true as Euclid. In
his "Hamburg Dramaturgy" Lessing said:
"I do not hesitate to confess (even if in
these enlightened times I am to be laughed
out of countenance for it) that I hold the
*Poetics* to be infallible as Euclid's Elements." And not so very long before
Lessing's time, Dacier had objected to
some one who had ventured to set up the
Bible against Aristotle: "As if Divinity
and the Holy Scriptures could ever be contrary to the sentiments of Nature on which
Aristotle founds his judgment!" This was
only giving another form to Roger Bacon's
observation that "Aristotle hath the same
authority in philosophy as the Apostle Paul
hath in divinity." So that, after all, it was
not so very much of a farcical exaggeration
when Racine in *Les Plaideurs* made an

advocate attempt to browbeat the bench with the authority of Aristotle in a case of fowl-stealing. Why, in one of the liveliest literary controversies of 1902, Mr. Churton Collins, another scholarly critic, singled out some criterion of Aristotle's, and said we must apply it "to all drama of classical quality." Now this is flying in the face of Aristotle himself. For Aristotle, throughout the *Poetics*, was professedly examining a particular species of tragedy at a certain stage of its growth. Matthew Arnold, in his preface to *Merope*, brings out this point in his own delightful, easy way. "The laws of Greek tragic art," says Arnold, "are not exclusive; they are for Greek dramatic art itself, but they do not pronounce other modes of dramatic art unlawful. . . . 'Tragedy,' says Aristotle, in a remarkable passage, 'after going through many changes, got the nature which suited it, and then it stopped. Whether or no the kinds of tragedy are yet exhausted,' he presently adds, 'tragedy being considered either in itself, or in respect to the stage, I shall not now inquire.' Travelling in a certain path, the spirit of man arrived at Greek tragedy; travelling in other paths, it may arrive at other kinds of tragedy."

Well, the spirit of man has, in fact, arrived at other kinds of tragedy, so that we must now resign ourselves to the historical view of Aristotle's *Poetics*. It will be our business, then, to consider some of his leading ideas as relative to the conditions of his time, and to trace the ups-and-downs of their course through the shifting conditions of later times. By this means we ought to get at any rate a bird's-eye view of what dramatic criticism has been in the past, and we may thus hope to be in a better position to ask how precisely it stands at the present day.

# III

## OLD AND NEW CRITICISM

# III

First, then, Aristotle's general point of view, the whole mood in which he approached art was, in an important respect, quite unlike ours. For Aristotle, mighty intellect though his was, could not let his intellect play *in vacuo*. He was a man of his time, and his time was not, like ours, a time wherein a clear distinction is seen between nature and art, between the practical and the æsthetic. To-day the æsthetic mood and the practical mood are very different. We have had a Schopenhauer to tell us that art marks off for us the world as idea from the world as will; it is life purged of the will-to-live. The æsthetic mood is a disinterested mood, and the feelings excited by a work of art—so far as art is directly concerned—are ends in themselves, enjoyed for their own sake, without the sequel of action, their natural sequel in real life.  In one of the Goncourt novels—*Manette Salomon*—there is the incident of a model, posing before a room full of art-students for what Trilby called "the altogether," who was suddenly covered with confusion by the sight of a stranger peeping in at the window.  The students were nothing to the model, who knew that they were in the æsthetic, the "disinterested" mood, just as though they were copying a statue; the Peeping Tom, however, would be in the very different mood of real life.  Even to-day there are people who treat art just as they treat reality, because they are incapable of the æsthetic mood.  Thomas Love Peacock in "Crotchet Castle" alludes to what was then the recent case of a cheesemonger who had broken the plaster-cast of a Venus over the head of its itinerant vendor.  What was more, the Justice of the Peace sided with him.  There are some remote circles where novels, all novels, are still accounted wicked because they speak of things untrue, that is, which have not actually happened.  Now this, or something like this, was the common atti-

tude of Greek criticism. To the Greek
art really was second nature; an inferior,
because a copied, a second-hand nature.
He applied the same moral criteria in-
differently to art and real life, the image
and the object. Hence Greek criticism,
being always coloured by this moralistic
tinge, differed strangely from ours. Solon
is said to have asked Thespis, that very
early actor - manager, how he could tell
so many lies before so many people.
For Plato stories, in our own sense,
were "stories" in what is still at times
the nursery sense, that is, fibs. There
was the same confusion of thought in
Aristotle, so that the modern reader is
constantly feeling *dépaysé*. Why, he asks
himself, must the hero of a tragedy be
neither very good nor very bad? Why
must his fate be determined by error and
not by wickedness? Why ought the
culminating fatality of a tragedy to be the
work of ignorance, and its true nature only
to be discovered afterwards? What are
we to make of such a distinction as this
between tragedy and comedy—that the

latter aims at representing worse people,
and the former better people, than those
of present reality? It is the moralistic
attitude, the absence of the disinterested
æsthetic mood, which explains these myste-
ries. Aristotle would have ruled out not
only Iago and Richard III. but Cordelia
and Desdemona.

This was what came of identifying art
with practical life. Nowadays we have
got so far from this point of view as, in
certain moods, to consider practical life as
an æsthetic spectacle, as a more intense
kind of art than art itself. Thus Burke
says a playhouse where the best tragedy
was being acted would at once be emptied
by the news that a state-execution was
about to take place in the adjoining square.
And Renan talks of all life as an æsthetic
spectacle: "This universe is a spectacle
which the Deity offers Himself; let us
carry out the intentions of the great
Choregus in contributing to make the spectacle as brilliant, as varied as possible."

These ideas of Aristotle, I say, seem to
us moderns very strange. And they seemed

strange, but not so strange, when tragedy
was "hatched again," and "hatched different," as Mrs. Poyser would put it, in France.
They seemed strange to Corneille, who dis-
cussed the *Poetics* with great acumen.  At
that time—and in that place—it would
have been impious to assert flatly that
Aristotle was wrong; all that people could
venture to contend was that his meaning
had been wrongly interpreted.  Did I not
say that every generation re-fashions the
classics for itself?  And so you have Corneille, troubled by the Aristotelian *dictum*
that the morals of the tragic hero must
be good, unable to hide the fact that many
of his own tragic heroes and heroines in-
fringed this law—you have Corneille giving
a new interpretation to the word " good."
By " good morals," he says, Aristotle must
have meant " the brilliant and lofty character of a virtuous or vicious nature, according as that nature is proper and suitable
to the personage."   In other words, " good "
meant any appropriate character, so long
as it was marked by tragic dignity.  You
will see that this was to empty Aristotle's

law of all its moral content.　In like manner
Corneille sought to turn Aristotle's position
that the tragic hero must not be entirely
good, that people must not be made to
suffer on the stage through no fault of
their own.　But—here is something to
show the persistency of Aristotelian ideas—
nearly a century after Corneille you have
Lessing protesting against his attempt to
warp the meaning of Aristotle, and reassert-
ing that the spectacle of an entirely good
character brought to woe was what Aristotle called it—μιαρόν, shocking.　And if
you want a still later instance of this view,
you have it in the case of the old Sheriff
of Dumbarton known to Louis Stevenson,
who could not bear even to read *Othello*.
"That noble gentleman . . . that noble
lady . . . too painful for me !"

　A more vigorous offshoot from this ethical criticism of the Greeks was the notion
that drama ought to aim at directly incul-
cating a moral.　This notion permeated all
eighteenth-century commentary and a good
deal of eighteenth-century practice.　Thus
Johnson praised *Timon of Athens* because

"the catastrophe affords a very powerful
warning against ostentatious liberality";
and he hinted some dispraise of *As You Like
It* because " by hastening to the end of the
work, Shakespeare suppressed the dialogue
between the usurper and the hermit, and
lost an opportunity of exhibiting a moral
lesson, in which he might have found matter
worthy of his highest powers." Johnson also
preferred Tate's *Lear* to Shakespeare's—
Tate, you may remember, gave Cordelia's
story a happy ending—because it showed
"the final triumph of persecuted virtue."
But the great champion of the didactic, or
hortatory, drama was Diderot, who wrote:
"It is always virtue and virtuous people
that a man ought to have in view when he
writes. Oh, what good would men gain
if all the arts of imitation possessed one
common object, and were one day to unite
with the laws in making us love virtue and
hate vice!" And so in his *Père de Famille*
Diderot introduces a father who addresses
his daughter thus: "Marriage, my daughter, is a vocation imposed by heaven. . . .
If marriage exposes us to cruel pain, it

is also the source of the sweetest pleasures.
. . . O sacred bond, if I think of thee, my
whole soul is warmed and elevated." " But
these virtuous ejaculations," says Mr. John
Morley—from whose volume on Diderot
I have borrowed this quotation, and upon
whose comment it would be presumptuous
in me to attempt any improvement—" these
virtuous ejaculations do not warm and
elevate us.   In such a case words count
for nothing.   It is actual presentation of
beautiful character, and not talk about it,
that touches the spectator.   It is the asso-
ciation of interesting action with character
that moves and inspires such better moods
as may be within our compass.   Diderot,
like many other people before and since,
sought to make the stage the great moral
teacher.   That it may become so is possible.
It will not be," concludes Mr. Morley, " by
imitating the methods of that colossal type
of histrionic failure, the church-pulpit ! "
Allusion to the church pulpit reminds one
that the Rev. Jeremy Collier, in his " Short
View of the Immorality and Profaneness of
the English Stage," laid it down that " the

business of plays is to recommend virtue
and discountenance vice." This moralistic
position need not surprise us in a clergy-
man. But what is surprising is that a man
like Vanbrugh, in his reply to Collier,
should have accepted this position as a
matter of course. It never occurred to
him to say, with Falstaff, " I deny your
major"; all that he could find to say was:
" What I have done is in general a dis-
couragement to vice and folly; I am sure
that I intended it, and I hope I have per-
formed it." So you see that Lamb's defence
of the Restoration drama on the ground
that it was unreal, a sort of fairy tale, something to which the ethical criteria of actual
life were irrelevant, could never have occurred to the Restoration dramatists themselves. With Lamb you have at least
reached the very opposite pole to the
moralistic criticism of Aristotle. You have
reached un-moralistic criticism.

For a still more striking piece of evidence
that modern thought cannot get away from
Aristotle—that criticism may be with him
or may be against him but cannot ignore

him—take the Aristotelian dictum about the relative importance of character and plot. There was a great to-do over this in the summer of 1902. The trouble began with a statement of a *Quarterly* reviewer about the essential thing in drama. "The essential thing in drama," said he, "is that the drama should be based on character, that the actions should be made by the characters." This remark "drew" several scholastic critics, who sought to floor the reviewer with the *Poetics*, as Johnson is said to have knocked down Osborne the bookseller with a folio. Here is the Aristotelian text:—

"Tragedy is an imitation, not of men, but of an action and of life. . . . Dramatic action, therefore, is not with a view to the representation of character; character comes in as subsidiary to the action. Hence the incidents and the plot are the end of a tragedy; and the end is the chief thing of all. Again, without action there cannot be a tragedy; there may be without character. . . . The plot, then, is the first principle, and, as it were, the soul of a tragedy ; character holds the second place."

Now the scholastic critics I have alluded to one and all argued as though this passage meant that character-development was less artistically important, less interesting, than plot-weaving; and there, I humbly think, they were all wrong.  I venture to submit to you a very different interpretation of this passage, a sense in which Aristotle's words are absolutely valid for all drama in all time.  It is that Aristotle here was not attempting an artistic appreciation at all, but making a scientific classification.  He was marking off the special province of drama in the general region of art.  The *differentia* of drama, what makes it itself and not something else, he shows, is action. If it were not action but character, then the "Caractères" of La Bruyère would be drama, and the description of the Club in the opening numbers of the *Spectator* would be drama, and Elia's sketch of George Dyer would be drama.  But characters are isolated forces, forces *in vacuo*.  To make drama these forces must come into collision ;

mathematically speaking, drama is a department of kinetics, not of statics. In other words, Aristotle is only anticipating M. Brunetière's consideration of drama as the struggle of a will against obstacles. And the proof, says Aristotle, is that you cannot have drama without action, though you may without character. Melodrama—that is, mechanical tragedy — presents action without character. And there are not wanting dullards who would contend that the opposite case, character without action, is illustrated by some plays of Ibsen. These are the people who are for ever talking as though action must be something external and strepitous; they are not satisfied unless the hero smashes the furniture or the heroine pushes her husband down a well. But these people were answered long ago, once and for all, by Dryden, a very great dramatic critic—in some respects, I almost think, the greatest since Aristotle—and I am not forgetting Lessing, for while Dryden's erudition equalled Lessing's, his criticism is more robust, more mundane, less academic. . . .

proceeds to illustrate
*Iphigenia.* Now, to-
be held that the pl
Aristotle's remarks h
originates and grow:
mind in all sorts of v
far from being the
worst, way. Is not
then finding characte
the soldier's recipe
—first you make a h
gun-metal round it?
son, however, seems
possibility. He once
biographer, that a nc
plot and find charac
might reverse the p
might take a certain
both persons and a
Yes, the novelist—or
any one of these th
choice is not, I fancy
ence. What—to tak
what is the secret (
impression left by s(
(or so-called problem

I wish I could have dwelt upon Dryden, not merely upon that wonderful thing of which I have already spoken, the *Essay of Dramatic Poesy*, with its exquisite little "impressionist" vignettes, its spirited dialectic, its noble liberality of taste, but also upon those critical defences, dedications, discourses, parallels, accompanying his plays, and now so much more valuable to us than, with scarce an exception, the plays themselves. But I could not, within my prescribed limits; it came to a choice between Aristotle and Dryden, and about that choice there could be no hesitation. . . . Well, Dryden effectually answered the people who talk as though action must be something external. "Every alteration," says one of the interlocutors in his great *Essay*—"every alteration or crossing of a design, every new-sprung passion, and turn of it, is a part of the action, and much the noblest, except we conceive nothing to be action till the players come to blows." This spiritual plot, this internal will-conflict, these soul-adventures, were all comprised in the Aristotelian "action."

If mor
it may a
some ma
blank lea
marks on
—which
rick, who
"Life of
tions—D
the fable
*quoad fu*
a pithy c
vanced th
place to p
appreciati

If Aris
scientific
well. Un
he subseq
very quee
Plot, it s
of compo
says, "wl
made or c
first sketc
in the epi

the feeling that the playwright has first thought of his thesis, his subject, his action as Aristotle would say, and has then fitted his characters to it? He has aimed at proving a case by manufacturing the evidence, and at the same time has spoiled our illusion by an obviously artificial pattern, something too symmetrical for resemblance to what Mr. Henry James calls "the strange irregular rhythm of life."

Why Aristotle overstated the case for plot, as compared with character, is a point not, I dare say, beyond conjecture. One may hazard the speculation that, in the actual life of his age, incidents, adventures, all the raw material of plot, fell more frequently within the experience of even the average man than they fall now. The "revolutions" and "discoveries" of Greek tragedy which are now relegated to melodrama — the long-lost heir, the "strawberry-mark," and all the rest of it —were not then by any means improbable. On the other hand, human character cannot then have been the complex thing it has since become. Further, it is quite possible that Aristotle detected a tendency in the tragedy of his day which he held dangerous to its vitality — the tendency to the merely statuesque, to sheer immobility. If so, his over-statement of the case for the other side was nothing else than a piece of that practical wisdom which we call opportunism. Even to-day the drama of motionless life has beguiled some men to heresy; M. Maeterlinck made it his ideal in his " Static Theatre "—the very negation of all drama.

And now let us turn to an Aristotelian point which has quite another kind of interest for us—an interest arising not from any queer application of it, but from its curious, its almost total, neglect. Aristotle mentions two ways of judging tragedy—in itself and in relation to the stage (πρὸς τὰ θέατρα). By τὰ θέατρα he means the audience as well as the " boards "—the whole " house," as we should say, before and behind the curtain. Now dramatic criticism in general, and Shakespearian criticism in particular, has been continuously vitiated by the neglect to consider

drama πρὸς τὰ θέατρα, in relation, that is,
to the practical conditions of the stage
and the audience.  Corneille complained
of the misrepresentations of Aristotle by
scholars who were ignorant of the playhouse; and this particular ignorance has
been equally fatal to an adequate interpretation of dramatic history.  Only one
conspicuous critic in the past has given
full recognition to this important side of
the question, and that is a man of the
Italian Renaissance, Lodovico Castelvetro.
Castelvetro's main points[1] were that not
only the form, but the content of the
drama was conditioned by the fact that it
is something transacted in a public place
before a motley crowd upon a circum-
scribed space within a limited time.  He
drew certain conclusions, with which we
need not trouble ourselves because they
are now out of date; his interest for us
is that he had the right method; the root
of the matter was in him.  On the other
hand, to this day you will find critics in-

[1] See *A History of Literary Criticism in the Renaissance*,
by Joel Elias Springarn (New York, 1899), p. 72.

terpreting Shakespeare's plays, and con-
trasting them with modern plays, without
any consideration of the stage and the
audience which Shakespeare had to write
for, or of the difference between the stage
and the audience as they were then and
as they are now. They take exclusively
the bookman's view.

Thus you will find a University Professor
deliberately telling us we must appreciate
Shakespeare by the text alone. "We
may be sure," he says, "that if we have
the wit to see it, we shall find in the text
the key to every problem which the story
may suggest." Just apply this precious
principle to solving the question why so
much of the Shakespearian text ignores
what we should now call the law of
dramatic economy, does not help on the
action, but consists of moral reflections,
apologues, speeches "improving the occasion." Examples of this element of the
old drama — which in the Aristotelian
analysis is called διάνοια — are Hamlet's
moralising on drunkenness, while he is
waiting for the ghost, his lecture on act-

ing to the players, Polonius' advice to
Laertes, and Jacques' Seven Ages speech.
Well, I defy our University Professor or
any one else adequately to explain why
this element in Shakespeare and the other
Elizabethans has disappeared in modern
drama, or to indicate when it disappeared,
without consideration of a certain little
change in the mechanical conditions of
the stage—namely, the gradual disappearance of the "apron." The "apron" is
the technical name for the stage-area in
front of the curtain. In the Elizabethan
theatre it jutted right out among the
public, who surrounded it on three sides.
This "apron" slowly shrank—Colley Cibber
writes that it was shortened by 10 feet in
his time [1]—till at last in our day it has
altogether disappeared, and the drama has
withdrawn within the frame of the pro-
scenium. While the apron existed you had
a platform-drama, rhetorical recitation in
costume, instead of the actual representa-

---

[1] When Rich altered the structure of Drury Lane in order
to get more room for his pit.  See *Life of Thomas Betterton,*
by R. W. Lowe (London, 1891), p. 27.

tion of our modern picture-drama. The
" apron " was like the shagreen skin in
Balzac's story; as it shrank, the life of
the old rhetoric-drama drew so much nearer
to its end. The disappearance of the
" apron" is of course not the only cause
of difference between Elizabethan and
modern drama; but a cause it is, and an
important one. Our " bookmen " have
overlooked it, because they cannot be got
to consider the drama, in Aristotle's phrase,
πρὸς τὰ θέατρα, in relation to the actual circumstances of the theatre.

It would be easy to multiply examples
of the "bookman's" besetting sin: his in-
corrigible habit of explaining plays by
play-books or books about plays without
reference to playhouses and playgoers.
There is, for instance, that famous appeal
to the imagination of the audience in the
" Chorus" speeches of *Henry V.*, in which
the " bookmen" represent Shakespeare as
talking *at* the " classic" critics of that day,
the strict Unitarians of Place and Time,
whereas we, I think, looking at the actual
scenic conditions of the Elizabethan stage,

with its unchanging background, and at the
actual mental condition of the Elizabethan
audience, which in mobility, in detachment, was very different from ours—looking, I say, at these conditions of the
time, we should, I think, find that Shakespeare was not wasting his breath by talking at anybody, but was trying to mitigate
a very real difficulty, to talk over a very
real recalcitrancy in his public. Then,
again, there is the question of the fights,
and wrestling - matches, and slaughterings
in Shakespeare's plays—in all Elizabethan
drama—which the " bookmen " put down
to some deliberate artistic preference in
the playwright; whereas we, I think, looking at the playhouse and its circumstances,
shall have to say they were there because
the Elizabethan public insisted upon them,
and insisted upon them for no æsthetic
reason whatever, but just because it was
accustomed to them, sometimes on that
very spot—on theatrical off-nights—and at
other times in the playing-fields just out-
side. It would be easy, I repeat, to

multiply examples of commentary running
wild for lack of that controlling principle
mentioned by Aristotle, the principle of
considering the drama πρὸς τὰ θέατρα. But
I will not proceed with any such multi-
plication; for it is time to have done with
Aristotle and his *Poetics*. If I have dwelt
so long on that masterpiece, it was that I
might bring out the element of permanence
in the history of criticism, the fact that it
has dealt through the ages with the same
sort of questions, always having them in
its mind—though perpetually changing its
mind about them. I must, however, en-
treat your indulgence for one more reference to a Greek—a successor of Aristotle—
merely a passing reference, because this
later Greek, though he occasionally touched
upon dramatic *diction*, did not deal with
drama; but a reference which is obligatory,
because he offers a kind of criticism very
different from Aristotle's, and above all
things different in that it can with pro-
priety be called "modern." I refer to
Longinus, whom Dryden calls (in his

"Apology for Heroic Poetry") "undoubtedly, after Aristotle, the greatest critic
among the Greeks." Aristotle had been
a pioneer, an explorer; he had mapped
out the country. His great business was
classification; he was the first of scientific
critics. But Longinus, as I say, was of
a different sort. Precisely of what sort
Longinus was you may learn from a note
in Gibbon's Diary for 3rd October 1762:
"Till now," says Gibbon, "I was acquainted only with two ways of criticising
a beautiful passage, the one to show by
an exact anatomy of it the distinct beauties
of it, and whence they sprang; the other,
an idle exclamation, or general encomium,
which leaves nothing behind it. Longinus
has shown me that there is a third. He
tells me his own feelings upon reading it;
and he tells them with such energy that
he communicates them." Longinus, then,
narrated the adventures of his soul among
masterpieces, he set down his impressions; he was the first of impressionist
critics. That character at once brings him
alongside an Anatole France or a Jules

Lemaître ; it carries us into the thick of " modernity." [1]

Gibbon, as you have seen, divided critics into three classes, and a great contemporary of Gibbon's also divided them into three. Johnson told Fanny Burney—who records it in her diary — that " There are three distinct kinds of judges upon all new authors or productions ; the first are those who know no rules, but pronounce entirely from their natural taste and feelings ; the second are those who know, and judge by rules ; and the third are those who know, but are above the rules. These last," said Johnson, " are those you should wish to satisfy. Next to these rate the natural judges ; but ever despise those opinions that are formed by the rules." Now I shall take leave to reduce these three classes to two ; for the first class, those people who knowing no rules are at the mercy of their undisciplined taste, do not concern us here ;

---

[1] For the " impressionism" of Longinus see Professor Saintsbury's " History of Criticism," vol. ii. p. 373 (London, 1902). Mr Andrew Lang in his Introduction to Mr. H. L. Havell's translation of Longinus on the Sublime (London, 1899) takes a somewhat different view.

they are not critics, in our sense of the term, at all. There remain, then, two classes of critics. On the one hand, there are those who judge by "the rules," by a code of orthodox canons and standards, by some law of taste external to their own, and independent of it. On the other hand, there are those who, while they have informed and fortified and purified their taste by the preliminary discipline of study —study of the works satisfying orthodox standards, study of "the rules"—nevertheless form their opinions upon no external laws of taste, but upon the report brought to them by their own taste, their own sensations and impressions. These are the two chief schools of criticism to-day—the brunt of the battle is between them—the "dogmatic" critics and the "impressionist" critics. In the process of comparing[1] these two schools we may perhaps find that there is not so much difference between them as they themselves suppose.

[1] For some points in the comparison I am indebted to M. Émile Faguet; Feuilleton of the *Journal des Débats* for 20th June 1896.

The "dogmatic" critic is by temperament an "intellectual." Understanding, not feeling, is his point. He does not share his feelings with us, as Gibbon said Longinus did, but his ideas. There is the possibility of ample pleasure for us in that, but it is an intellectual pleasure—the pleasure given by a symmetrical or strictly logical ordering of ideas, by subtle disquisition, by what the mathematicians call a "neat" or an "elegant" demonstration. The pleasure for the critic of this sort is to classify, and to compare. Such-and-such a play belongs to this or that dramatic family, or holds a certain rank in the dramatic hierarchy. *Hamlet*, being a tragedy, is "nobler," as Aristotle would have said, than *Much Ado*, a comedy. Or you will be shown the "periodicity" of dramatic motives: how *Hamlet* is largely a modern *Oresteia*, how the *Adelphi* of Terence reappears as *A Pair of Spectacles*. Or the play, morally considered, belongs to a wholesome, or a pernicious, or a frivolous class. It is always a classification this critic gives you, a classification to accord with general ideas

of art, or sociology, or ethics; every work
this critic sees he sees *through* his general
idea.  He is judging—First Prize, Class A;
Second Prize, Class B; Proxime Accessit
or "Ploughed"—judging, not feeling.

But if he does chance to have feelings—
and even this temperament can hardly
escape them altogether—he regards his
feelings with distrust.  You seem to over-
hear him saying to himself: "I like this
play, therefore I am prompted to call it
good; but my general ideas tell me it
belongs to a bad class, therefore I must
call it bad.  Evidently then, despite the
evidence of my senses, I can't really like
it."  And the good man, flushed with the
pride of a victory over self, a mortification
of the flesh, loudly damns the play to
drown the last echoes of his own spon-
taneous, human feelings.

To reinforce his judgments—for judicial
decisions must have the sanction of something external to the judge—he calls in
tradition, the "rules."  This undoubtedly
gives him an air of authority.  He seems
to be broad-based upon the people's will;

he comes before us not as himself, but as
the representative of a "thumping majority."
That is the dogmatic critic.

The "impressionist" critic has greater
interest in his feelings and less confidence
in his general ideas and external authority.
His fundamental principle is the fact that
we are all, whether we know it or not, shut
up within ourselves. It was in answering
M. Brunetière, who has constituted himself
the champion—and a very doughty champion—of the dogmatists, that M. Anatole
France insisted upon this fundamental
principle. "There is no objective criticism
any more than there is objective art, and
all those who flatter themselves that they
put something else than themselves into
their work are the dupes of the cheapest
illusion. The truth is, we never get out
of ourselves. That is one of our greatest
miseries. What would we not give for
one minute to see heaven and earth with
the facetted eye of a fly, or to compre-
hend nature with the rude and simple brain
of an orang-outang? But that is denied
to us. We cannot, like Tiresias, be a

man and yet remember we have been a woman. We are shut up in our own person as in some perpetual prison-house. The best thing we can do, it occurs to me, is to recognise this frightful limitation with a good grace, and to confess that we are speaking of ourselves — whenever we have not the strength to hold our tongues." Now there is of course some exaggeration here — or rather, some mis-direction. As M. Brunetière had no diffi-culty in showing, M. France has drawn the red herring of metaphysics across the track. The fact that the external universe is only known through the Ego does not prevent normally constituted men from arriving at a common judgment about in-numerable things in the universe. M. France's argument, in fact, proves too much ; it would invalidate not only ob-jective criticism, but all history, all science. At the same time it proves too little, for it covers only our personal contribution to an act of criticism, it leaves out the contribution of the ages, the " something not ourselves."

Nevertheless, this self-concentration, or introspective habit, of the "impressionist" critic has the supreme merit of genuineness, of veracity. The great drawback of so-called "objective" criticism is its tendency to self-deception, to say nothing of hypocrisy. We take judgments on trust instead of testing them by our actual experience. We cheat ourselves of our pleasures, out of fear of some external prohibition, or else we fool ourselves into thinking we like a work, when in reality we do not, just because we suppose that according to "the rules" we ought to like it. To this very common attitude of mind there is a characteristic reference by Dickens in one of his letters written to Forster from Venice. Dickens says how necessary it is for a man "to overcome the villainous meanness of professing what other people have professed when he knows (if he has capacity to originate an opinion) that his profession is untrue. The intolerable nonsense against which genteel taste and subserviency are afraid to rise, in connexion with art, is astounding." . . . (You are told) "on pain of being broke for want of gentility in appreciation, to go into ecstasies ; . . . you immediately obey, and tell your son to obey. He tells his son, and he tells his, and so the world gets at three-fourths of its frauds and miseries." Well, our safeguard against these frauds and miseries is " impressionist " criticism. The " impressionist " takes a pure natural joy in his own sensations, because they are his own. He declines to be " connoisseured out of his senses." He asks himself, " Do I really like this work ? Whether it pleased my great-grandfathers or not—does it please me ? And if it does, then I cannot explain my pleasure to others —in Gibbon's phrase about Longinus, tell my feelings with such energy that I communicate them—unless I explain myself, my temperament." And so the " impressionist " is committed to an analysis of self, to the psychology of the Ego. He " narrates the adventures of his soul."

Thereupon there is often a shrill outcry against him. Egoist ! Where is your modesty ? Keep yourself to yourself ! Thus at a Congress of Journalists in 1902 a veteran provincial editor, lecturing the dramatic critics upon their duties—a popular pastime — sternly enjoined absolute silence about the Ego. Well, I cannot but think that those who raise this cry misunderstand the very nature of criticism. I waive the point that the real immodesty lies not with those who pretend to speak only for themselves, but with those who profess to speak in the general name. I waive the point that the reader often objects to " egoism " in the critic merely because it offends his own egoism, because there is a collision of *amours propres*. I waive the plea for autobiographic criticism which is included in the plea for autobiography at large—that it is, as Sir Leslie Stephen says, the one subject upon which the writer happens to be the highest living authority. But the fact remains that to give an account of your impressions without any account of the temperament which has been impressed, is to withhold from your reader an essential piece of evidence for enabling him to form his own judgment about them. The value of your impressions will depend upon your

approximation to that ideal consumer of
art, described at the outset of this inquiry,
ὁ χαρίεις of Aristotle; it is for you to
provide your reader with the necessary
materials for making up his mind about
you; you must produce your credentials.

And your "authority" with the reader?
It will not be found in an external set of
laws, traditions, "the rules"; it will be in
the delicacy, the fineness, the distinction, of
your impressions. They are for the reader
to take or to leave. He may say: "No, I
don't feel like that, but comparison of my
own feelings with this man's has helped me
to realise my own pleasure more clearly";
or he may say: "Yes, that is what I
vaguely feel, the knowledge of this man's
feelings has illuminated, expanded, warmed,
and invigorated my own." There is the
critic's "authority"—the interest, the "use"
of criticism.

And now, after this contrast of the two
opposed schools of criticism, it is time to
warn you that it has only been made for
the sake of clearing up our ideas and must
not be taken too seriously. Unmitigated

dogmatism, absolute impressionism—there
are no such things.  Your most hardened
dogmatist is at times an impressionist—at
times when he is driven in upon himself,
when his classifications, his references to
general principles, break down, and he is
left to speak for himself, to say, "I am so
constituted that I cannot help liking this or
disliking that"—"I do not like thee, Dr.
Fell, But why it is I cannot tell."  After
all, his general classifications are subjective,
for the simple reason that no two critics
have ever chosen exactly the same set.
And so it is with the most independent
impressionist ; he cannot — whatever M.
France may say — isolate himself from
humanity, from the ambient air, from the
mass of literary tradition and dogma and
the code of artistic right and wrong, better
and worse, which is the heritage from our
fathers that begat us.  In either kind of critic
it all comes back in the last resort to a
question of temperament ; whether they be
impressionists or dogmatists, it is in virtue
of their temperament, the true inwardness
of them, that they please and persuade us.

It is by their temperament that we shall rank the men of either kind, or refuse to rank them, among the elect of criticism—"the *judices natos*," as Dryden calls them (in his Dedication of the Æneid) : "souls of the highest rank and truest understanding. These," says he, "are few in number ; but whoever is so happy as to gain their approbation can never lose it, because they never give it blindly. Then they have a certain magnetism in their judgment, which attracts others to their sense. Every day they gain some new proselyte, and in time become the Church." When we clearly perceive that ideal of good criticism, we can all I think assent to what Tennyson said, almost on his deathbed—"Good critics are rarer than good authors."

But Tennyson said, at an earlier time, something else, something which points to a limitation of even the best criticism and to an excuse for even the worst authors. Some one had quoted to him a prayer of Jowett's, praying that we might see ourselves as others see us. "No," replied Tennyson, "I should not pray for that :

others cannot see much of one's inner self."
Criticism should always allow for that; it
cannot pierce to the author's inmost self.
Life is so obscure a thing that there is a
sense in which all criticism is futile and
impertinent.   Who can plumb the ocean of
thought and feeling of which any man's
written words are but the surface-foam?
The artist abandons himself, in Goethe's
phrase, to his *dæmon;* what may seem to us
failures, incongruities, are but necessary
parts of an inward and spiritual harmony
of the man, which remains hidden from us.
And so, as M. Paul Bourget says in speaking of Amiel, "There is in every productive
energy something mysterious and sacred,
which it behoves us to consider as above
discussion and judgment."

THE END

Printed by BALLANTYNE, HANSON & Co.
Edinburgh & London

# THE WORKS OF LORD BYRON

A New Text, Collated with the Original MSS. and Revised Proofs, which are still in existence, with many hitherto unpublished additions. This will be the most complete Edition of Lord Byron's Works, as no other Editors have had access to the original MSS. With Portraits and Illustrations. To be completed in 13 Vols. Crown 8vo, 6s. each.

## POETRY. Edited by ERNEST HARTLEY COLERIDGE.

Vol.   I. THE EARLY POEMS.
Vol.  II. CHILDE HAROLD.
Vol. III. THE GIAOUR, BRIDE OF ABYDOS, CORSAIR, ETC.
Vol. IV. PRISONER OF CHILLON, MANFRED, BEPPO, MAZEPPA, VISION OF JUDGMENT, MARINO FALIERO, ETC.
Vol.  V. SARDANAPALUS, ETC.
Vol. VI. DON JUAN.
Vol. VII. EPIGRAMS, BIBLIOGRAPHY, INDEX, ETC.          [*Shortly.*

\*\*\* Owing to the extent of the Notes to Byron's Works, which contain a large amount of new information, it has been found impossible to include the whole in Six Volumes.

A Seventh Volume, containing occasional pieces, a bibliography, and a very full index of all Byron's Works, is in the press.

## LETTERS. Edited by ROWLAND E. PROTHERO, M.V.O.

| | |
|---|---|
| Vol.   I. 1788 to 1811. | Vol. IV. 1816 to 1820. |
| Vol.  II. 1811 to 1814. | Vol.  V. 1820 to 1822. |
| Vol. III. 1814 to 1816. | Vol. VI. 1822 to 1824. With Index. |

"The sixth volume of Byron's prose writings concludes one of the most attractive collections of letters and journals in the language, and one of the best edited works our literature possesses."—Dr. R. Garnett in the *Bookman*.

---

## IS IT SHAKESPEARE? The Great Question of

Elizabethan Literature, answered in the Light of New Revelations and important Contemporary Evidence hitherto unnoticed. By a CAMBRIDGE GRADUATE. With Facsimiles. Demy 8vo, 12s. net.

---

## NOVA SOLYMA, THE IDEAL CITY ; OR, JERUSALEM

REGAINED. An Anonymous Romance written in the Time of Charles I., 1628–1648. Now first drawn from obscurity, and attributed, by internal evidence, to the illustrious John Milton, author of "Paradise Lost." With Introduction, Translation, Literary Essays, and a Bibliography. By the Rev. WALTER BEGLEY. 2 Vols. Demy 8vo, 21s. net.

"One of the most astonishing works that has been produced for years."
—*Daily Telegraph.*

LONDON : JOHN MURRAY, ALBEMARLE STREET, W.

**OF AUCASSIN AND NICOLETTE.** A Translation in Prose and Verse from the Old French. Together with AMABEL AND AMORIS (now given for the first time). By LAURENCE HOUSMAN. With Illustrations by PAUL WOODROFFE. Engraved on Wood by CLEMENCE HOUSMAN. Crown 8vo, 5s. net.

---

**THE SAILING OF THE LONG-SHIPS, AND** OTHER POEMS. By HENRY NEWBOLT, Author of "Admirals All," "The Island Race," &c. Small crown 8vo, 2s. 6d. net.

"This volume will be acquired and valued by all who care for vigorous and tender verse."—*Globe.*

"Admirable verses . . . themes of patriotism expressed in lines of true poetry."—*St. James's Gazette.*

---

**WE ARE SEVEN.** Half-Hours on the Stage—Grave and Gay. By HAMILTON AÏDÉ, Author of "The Snares of the World." Crown 8vo, 4s. net.

---

## TO ALL LOVERS OF MUSIC

### MR. MURRAY'S MUSICAL SERIES

Crown 8vo, 5s. net each

**THE ORCHESTRA AND ORCHESTRAL** MUSIC. With Eight Portraits and other Illustrations.

**WHAT IS GOOD MUSIC?** Suggestions to Persons Desiring to Cultivate a Taste in Musical Art, and HOW MUSIC DEVELOPED. By W. J. HENDERSON.

**MUSIC:** How it Came to be What it Is. By HANNAH SMITH. With Illustrations.

**SONGS AND SONG WRITERS.** By HENRY T. FINCK. With Eight Portraits.

**THE OPERA, PAST AND PRESENT.** An Historical Sketch. By WILLIAM FOSTER APTHORP. With Portraits.

**CHOIRS AND CHORAL MUSIC.** By ARTHUR MEES. With Portraits.

**HOW TO LISTEN TO MUSIC.** Hints and Suggestions to Untaught Lovers of the Art. By HENRY EDWARD KREHBIEL. With Eleven Portraits.

LONDON: JOHN MURRAY, ALBEMARLE STREET, W.

OP IX 16ᵉ épreuve

6⁵⁰